Share your colored versions with us ! We love seeing your results and hearing from you.
we are social !

The Official FB book page, stay on top of what we have in the works !
www.facebook.com/AMWART
The Community group, share your colored pages, meet the artists, enjoy exclusive freebies, take part in community Charity books and so much more......
www.facebook.com/groups/fansandfriendsamwart
www.facebook.com/groups/ColorAWerdieADay
Follow us on Twitter..... @GlobalDoodlegem
We are on Instagram too
@globaldoodlegems for Instagram
...and if you are not social like that we have a blog
globaldoodlegems.wordpress.com

Copyright © 2019 Global Doodle Gems
All rights are reserved by Global Doodle Gems.
Duplication of pages for personal use are allowed. You are invited to color the pages then scan/post your coloured versions to social networks, mentioning the book title and author/artist (Global Doodle Gems).
All artwork and images are protected by copyright laws. This book or any portion thereof may not, otherwise, be reproduced and/or distributed or transmitted without the express written permission of the artist/publisher of Global Gems.
All of us from the Global Doodle Gems wish you a colortastic time and look forward to seeing your wonderful color results online !

A Heart A Day 2
366 book A Heart A Day vol. 2 Patterned Hearts... have fun and enjoy !

"This book is dedicated to the love of my life, my daughter Victoria Panthera. I make these books in hopes that your life as an adult will be everything you want It to be! I love you more than words can say!"

Maria Wedel

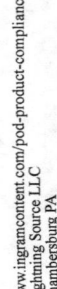